How To Get What You ꞯꜱꜱꝋ. ꜱ

Study Of The Magic Laws Of Nature

Alexander Cannon

Kessinger Publishing's Rare Reprints

Thousands of Scarce and Hard-to-Find Books
on These and other Subjects!

- Americana
- Ancient Mysteries
- Animals
- Anthropology
- Architecture
- Arts
- Astrology
- Bibliographies
- Biographies & Memoirs
- Body, Mind & Spirit
- Business & Investing
- Children & Young Adult
- Collectibles
- Comparative Religions
- Crafts & Hobbies
- Earth Sciences
- Education
- Ephemera
- Fiction
- Folklore
- Geography
- Health & Diet
- History
- Hobbies & Leisure
- Humor
- Illustrated Books
- Language & Culture
- Law
- Life Sciences
- Literature
- Medicine & Pharmacy
- Metaphysical
- Music
- Mystery & Crime
- Mythology
- Natural History
- Outdoor & Nature
- Philosophy
- Poetry
- Political Science
- Science
- Psychiatry & Psychology
- Reference
- Religion & Spiritualism
- Rhetoric
- Sacred Books
- Science Fiction
- Science & Technology
- Self-Help
- Social Sciences
- Symbolism
- Theatre & Drama
- Theology
- Travel & Explorations
- War & Military
- Women
- Yoga
- *Plus Much More!*

We kindly invite you to view our catalog list at:
http://www.kessinger.net

HOW TO GET WHAT YOU WANT

(A Study of the Magic Laws of Nature)

(Based upon a lecture given in the Renton Terrace Hall, Leeds, on Sunday, 6th October, 1912; at the Mayfair Hotel Tea-Talk on March 25th, 1934, and also delivered to the Bridlington Literary and Debating Society, January 23rd, 1934. Several interesting appendices appear at the end of this lecture, concerned with the various manifestations of thought-power which attended the occasion of the Mayfair lecture.)

A right attitude of mind is the key to the secret of success. A wrong attitude of mind is the instrument of what is called " Black Magic," and will bring into our lives, and into the lives of our associates, the evil imaginings of which we are the guilty harbourers. As the previous lecture has made clear, the world of sense, and space, and time, is a world of reflection: we and all about us are but the reflections in space-time of the eternal verities of the Godhead. We are like so many little cups of water in which the universal sun of God's spiritual nature is reflected. If we keep these little cups of water clean and clear we shall reflect a pure picture of the universal Good. But if we let the "water" in our "cups" become tainted and impure, then the image of God is distorted and faint.

It is by right-thinking that we keep these little cups of water pure and clean. And if we keep a watchful eye upon our conscious minds (the surface of the water in our little cups) we shall be able to prevent evil shapes from alighting thereon and, by natural action, sinking into the depths of our "cups"—our subconscious and unconscious minds—therein to ruin our lives and stifle our spiritual natures.

CHAPTER TWO

WHATSOEVER a man soweth, that shall he also reap.   So says the Bible in the seventh verse of the sixth chapter of the Book of Galatians.   How many Christians believe that with all their heart and soul?   The Christian West has always claimed the Bible to be full of Wisdom but it has never given the Bible real credit for being a book which can be relied upon and proven to the hilt as a scientific treatise.   Some people have, of course, relied upon it; but usually they have based their reliance upon a form of sentimentalism which has not succeeded in convincing others of the real virtues of the great book.   Perhaps there *is* a good deal in the Bible that is mere history, and perhaps some of it is *not* very pleasing history, but the fact remains that, underneath all this, and especially in the New Testament, there is a vast store of knowledge concerning the way in which life should be lived if a man or a woman is to get from life its true measure of satisfaction.

I claim it to be quite true that a man reaps whatsoever he sows, and that the passage in the Book of Proverbs which says *Keep thy heart with all diligence; for out of it are the issues of life,**

* Proverbs 4 : 23.

reveals the Ancients as being in possession of the knowledge of the sowing and reaping processes of life, and of the well-springs of disaster and of well-being which are to be found in our hearts.

You will notice in the Bible, that whenever it wishes to tell you to *guard* your thoughts or to *express* your innermost thoughts, it never speaks of guarding your *mind*, or of "keeping your *mind*," or of looking carefully into your *mind*. No, it always speaks of guarding your *heart*, or of keeping your *heart*, or of looking carefully into it. Now, there is a reason for this: it is not just a vague substitution of words. It means that the Ancients knew quite well that the faculty we call the mind is really the conscious mind, whereas the instrument *they* called the heart really meant the unconscious mind—the depths of your nature in which the power of your being is generated. It is there, in those deep springs of your nature, that the good or evil impulses of your life are bred. You had control of them once, when they were just passing flashes in your conscious mind, but you let them go unchallenged and unchecked, and they sank down into the unconscious, there to breed as a seed breeds when it is sown into the dark ground.

That is what sowing implies. It means the sowing of thought-seed into your own unconscious mind, and also the sowing of that thought-seed into the unconscious mind of the world. The one sowing you can do with your mind, but the other needs deeds also; those actions which speak louder than words.

Let us look at this sowing and reaping process in all its many aspects, for so many people are ignorant of these simple rules of life, and they go through life spreading good and evil thoughts around quite indiscriminately, thereby bringing havoc upon themselves and upon others. They are, as it were, not trained to be human beings. Unlike most animals, they have the power of directed conscious thought, but they have never learned to control that great power. They are, to quote the Poet's words,

Like little wanton boys that swim on bladders
. . . far beyond their depth.

They do not know that a knowledge of spiritual law is necessary to success in life, and that this law must be obeyed before it will become a man's servant. Obedience precedes authority, and the law obeys man when he obeys the law. The laws of electricity must be obeyed before the power of electricity is at man's disposal. If man misunderstands or misapplies the laws of electricity, then disaster is inevitable. So it is with the laws of the Universal Mind!

Remember that you are as a little cell in a huge body. The life of the body of mankind affects you, just as much as your life affects the body of mankind in turn. If you are not functioning properly, then to that extent you are affecting all the others in that body. If the body is not functioning properly because of some other cell's misbehaviour, then you feel the result. Think of the Great War! Think of the millions of innocent men, women and children who were horribly killed just because a section of men did not control their greedy, vain and murderous thoughts. That will show you how swift is the visitation of Nemesis upon those who hold evil thoughts, and also upon those who stand by and do nothing to check their growth.

For the law of life is a law of giving and getting. It is a law of action and reaction, and this implies that whatsoever a man may send out in thought, word, or deed, will return to him again. If he gives, he will receive. If he loves, he will be loved. If he praises, he will be praised. If, on the contrary, he hates, then he will find hatred. If he is harsh with others, he will live in a world full of harshness. Of course, he may not see his good or his evil returning to him *at once*; and many people have lost faith and have given up the fight when success was very near, because they did not know the meaning of the Biblical truth which promises reward to him that *endureth to the end.* *
Life is no game of chance as is so often believed. It is like a boomerang, rather, that comes back to the hand that flung it; or it may be likened to a hen that comes home to roost and trails her brood behind her.

---

* Matthew 10 : 22.

In the East this law is known as the law of *Karma* (meaning in the *Sanskrit* the law of "Come-back"). It is the law of the come-back or back-lash of your thoughts and deeds.

So many people still believe that they can separate thoughts, words, and deeds. How foolish is such a belief! To say one thing and to do another! To think one thing and to say the very opposite! How absurd, really! Did not Jesus, the great Nazarene Yogi, say: *Ye have heard that it was said by them of old time, Thou shalt not commit adultery: But I say unto you, That whosoever looketh on a woman to lust after her hath committed adultery with her already in his heart.**

In his heart. . . . Mark the words, and mark them well. Not just in his mind: not just a fleeting thought that could be forgotten, but a deep-seated and powerful thing that has its foul hand upon the control-lever of the body and can make it do things which would put to shame the apparent mastery of the mind.

A man accused of evil will sometimes admit his action, but excuse himself by saying: "I'm only following nature." This is no excuse at all, and it should be a punishable offence to leave the unconscious mind unguarded by the consciousness. Your unconscious mind must be watched and controlled by stopping evil thoughts in the conscious mind. Remember that it is not sufficient just to be good in a namby-pamby sort of way. Letting what is

* Matthew 5 : 27-38.

seemingly well alone does not always pay by any means. Your unconscious mind may not have been filled with deliberately evil thoughts by your conscious mind (you may be what is called "pure"), but all the time you may have been holding little nervous, fearful thoughts; or little mean thoughts, which like so many seeds dropping into the earth, have dropped into your unconscious mind and have peopled it with nervous, fearful and mean shapes.

I believe that if you do not run your own unconscious mind yourself, somebody else will run it for you. Hence the adage that the Devil will find plenty of work for idle hands to do. Such idleness can be a very real evil. We often sympathize with a person whose whole mentality has been eaten up with idleness when really we ought to shake him hard to bring him to a realization of his responsibility. This applies always to fear. No one *ought* to hold a fearful thought. It is not a matter for sympathy but for a warning; not a matter for weakness but for strength: for whereas we have been so apt to regard fear as a negative thing, it is actually a positive thing which creates the object of its own emotion. Fear is as dangerous as disease and ought to be fought with great power.

Let me give you some instances of the operation of fear in the mind and heart. Let me prove to you that what you fear will sooner or later materialize in your life. Then perhaps you will appreciate the great truth that fear is not passive, it is dynamic.

I knew a lady who feared an extremely rare disease. So terrified was she that she was continually living in dread of this disease, and bought every book she could find which made any reference to it. She feared it so much that she came at last to be gripped by a morbid fascination for the very thing she feared. Her end was dramatic. The disease, rare as it was, invaded her body and killed her. She had done with that disease just what I counselled you to do in the last lecture with a stone or a gem—she had held it in mind so tenaciously, and had concentrated upon it so effectively, that it had clothed itself with *Akhasa*, and the *Akhasa* in this case was her own body. She had controlled the *Mayâ* of her own body until it had manifested the illusion of disease. She died the victim of her own imagination. Just as I told you in the last lecture how to make yourself light with *Pranayama*, and how to cure diseases by holding the perfect picture of your patient in your mind, so this pitiful story demonstrates the reverse action—that of inflicting a disease upon yourself by fear.

Let me tell you of another case in point.

A man I knew who was worth thousands of pounds, was always joking about "getting ready for the workhouse" as he called it. He lived to repent his tragic joke, for as the years passed by his money vanished and he became almost destitute. He had so impressed the idea of poverty upon his unconscious mind that the Thought became the Thing.

A lady I know of was asked by a friend of mine during an epidemic if she had had the 'flu. "Not yet!" replied the lady brightly, thus indicating that she was expecting the illness, and that she was thereby preparing the way for the very thing she wished to avoid. Fear is at the root of all illness, for it checks the currents of vitality at their source. It lowers the *Prana.* Imagine the effect upon the men in a submarine if their commander, after looking through his periscope, told them that the waters up above were thick with enemy destroyers, and that they were utterly surrounded by nets and mines. Would they not be paralysed? Would they not think it better to give up the ghost, knowing that they dare not move because their engines would be overheard, that they dare not rise because they would be smashed, and that they could not stay where they were because of the slow death by suffocation. Can you not imagine the paralysing effect upon all their activities? They would be unable to do anything, because to them there would be no sense in doing anything. Life would suddenly seem a futile wait for death. Can you not imagine that this is just how the organs of the body feel when the brain, the instrument of the mind, sends down to them a cold blast of fear. Your organs cannot see anything outside the body: they have to believe what you tell them you can see in the outside world. If you see fear and danger, then your organs, like the submarine crew, will get depressed, and they will tend to miss the very chances of protection that otherwise they would have had.

Our bodies, like men under authority, need cheer and comfort. They are alive, you know, and not just lumps of fleshy machinery. They are sensitive living nations—millions upon millions of little cells all acting in their little way as tiny reflections, in tiny cups of water, of the Universal Spirit which you in turn reflect.

Therefore, give them courage, and give them hope. Dispel fear from them and lift the cold fingers of its inhibition from off their delicate functions. How can you do this? Why, it is simple. You must first KNOW YOURSELF, as the Greek philosophers commanded. You need to know that there is a perfect picture of yourself somewhere in your mind. It is perfect because you are a reflection of God, and the divine nature never makes anything imperfect. You must diligently seek after this perfect pattern which is hidden deep in your nature, and once it is found you must strive to mould your conscious life to its pattern. Those who do this need have no fear, for there is nothing to fear. The further you go on, the more you find yourself wishing with all your heart to live the right sort of life, the more you

will become sensitive to the still, small voice of
conscience within your soul, "heart," or unconscious mind. You will not, as so many do, look
upon this voice as a sort of alarum bell which
only rings when you are doing wrong, as though
the only job of a conscience is to prick its owner.
Instead, you will look upon it as the inner
compass which answers to the Poles of God.
You will begin to see that in following its
guidance you are developing your own inner
urge, and are fulfilling the perfect pattern of
yourself which is contained in your unconscious
mind. You will realize that your conscience
is the little "wireless receiver" by which you
receive the telepathic message of hope from the
great Universal Mind.

Let me now give you some examples of the
power of courage and of true faith to develop
the real God qualities which constitute the real
man, and also of its power to change one's
environment to keep in tune with the new
realization.

Let me tell you first of all about the young
man who came to me saying that all he pos-
sessed in the world were the forty shillings in his
pocket, that he was far from home, and that he
had no prospects in life. "What can *I* do to
change my condition?" he asked plaintively.

"Bless those forty shillings in your pocket," I
said. "By that means you will multiply them,
just as our Lord Jesus multiplied the loaves and
the fishes." I then explained to him that Christ

taught us that *everyone* has the power to bless and to multiply, to heal and to prosper. The forty shillings having been duly blessed, the young man was instructed to listen for his inner voice to tell him what to do. I told him that this was the telepathic guidance of his unconscious mind by the great Universal Mind, and that it was his unerring guide. After a while the young man said, "I feel I should like to go home." Now, his home was far away from London in the heart of the country: the train fare would absorb nearly all of his forty shillings; and there was no money in his home, nor work in the neighbourhood. Reason would have counselled him to stay in London and to look for work. However, when he told me how he felt about things, I commanded him to obey his inner voice (the dictator of his unconscious mind) and go back to his home, and I told him, moreover, that he must tell himself night and morning that the great Universal Mind would lead him into the way of prosperity. I told him that he could assert his claim upon his birthright, and that he could by divine right draw his own unto himself with an irresistible force, for God intended him to have all those things that were necessary to the fulfilment of his destiny. With these words I sent him on his journey.

For some weeks I heard nothing from him. Then one day I heard to the effect that a stranger had come to his village, had taken a fancy to him, and had almost at once put him in the way of earning several hundreds of pounds.

Another similar case was that of a man who rang me up to tell me that he had been summoned to pay five hundred pounds. "I haven't five hundred pence," he moaned, "and there is no way of getting any money either." I replied that there was a supply for every demand, I gave thanks to God that this man should receive the five hundred pounds, and I told the man to keep an unwavering faith in God and His goodness. However, the day drew near for the payment of the debt and no money was forthcoming. In desperation he rang me up to tell me that he was still without anything. It happened to be New Year's Day. "Don't worry," I advised him. "Nobody is going to issue a summons on you to-day. Pull yourself together! Act the part of a rich man! Show that you really believe what you say! If you do you will receive the money by to-morrow." He then asked me to dine with him that evening to help him keep his spirits up. When we met at the Ritz, I said to him: "Now, remember, this is no time to economize. Order a fine dinner. Act as though you had already received more than your five hundred pounds. Remember what it says in the twenty-second verse of the second chapter of Saint Matthew: *Whatsoever ye shall ask in prayer, believing, ye shall receive*; and don't forget to pay special attention to the word BELIEVING in the middle of that sentence. It is the *faith* that counts. And you have just got to prove it to be true by acting as though the money were *already* yours."

The next afternoon my friend was due to appear in court. He telephoned me at midday. "The money hasn't come," he lamented. "Why worry?" was my reply. "God is never late. He will take care of you. Remember the words of Isaiah: *And it shall come to pass, that before they call, I will answer.**

Well, it appears that at two o'clock in the afternoon, just as he was preparing to leave for the court, a wealthy relative dropped in to see him, and, upon hearing that he was called to court, and eliciting his financial state, sat down there and then and wrote him a cheque *for £50 more than the amount claimed from him.*

I may say frankly that I was a little relieved myself when I heard the news, for the man's faith was so weak and vacillating that he had actually delayed the gift by wasting his energies in fear and in preparing to attend the court. People *will* not realize that as the money is first made apparent upon the invisible plane, they must not jeopardize its manifestation on the visible plane by refusing to recognize it on the invisible one.

If you ask for success and at the same time prepare for failure you will get the situation

---

* Isaiah 65 : 24.

you have envisaged. Remember that it is not so much *what* you ask for, as *how you prepare for its reception* that counts. For mere words do not constitute prayer. *It is as a man thinketh in his heart . . . not in his mind.*

In other words, your actions are the real prayer. This being so, you must, if you would pray in real faith, prepare to receive the thing asked for when there is not the slightest sign of it in sight. When the three kings were in the desert without water, they consulted Elisha the prophet, and he said to them: *Thus saith the Law:* (mistranslated in the English Bible as Thus saith the Lord) *Make this valley full of ditches. Ye shall not see wind, neither shall ye see rain; yet that valley shall be filled with water.** They did so, you will remember, with the result that the rain came.

Apply this Law that Elisha demonstrated to your own life, and *according to your faith it shall be added unto you.* The thing cannot be done without a struggle. It is not going to be as easy as you might imagine. "*Just believe?*" you will say. "*How easy!*" Believe me, you are making a great mistake. It is easy to *say* that you believe, but it is another thing to have *real* faith, and believe with all your heart. All along at first you will encounter doubt: you will hear a voice saying, "Don't you believe it, old chap. *You* prepare for a rainy day. Take *my* advice and don't be a fool!" This is the voice of the

---

* 2 Kings 3 : 16-17.

Tempter, and you must answer it by saying, *Get thee behind me, Satan!* You must throw the thought out of your mind.

There isn't any big accomplishment in the world's history that was not brought to pass by courage allied to vision. There is hardly a victory that was not immediately preceded by a grim fear, for *the darkest hour precedes the dawn.* Just before the big achievement comes, things often look utterly hopeless, and apparent failure and discouragement appear in a formidable guise. But this, too, is a biblical truth. When the Children of Israel reached the Promised Land, they were afraid to go in, for they said, *And there we saw the giants... and we were in our own sight as grasshoppers.** Take particular notice that they said that they were *in their own sight* as grasshoppers. It was a question of self-imposed impotence. *They were impotent because they were afraid.* Everyone is impotent until he replaces his fears by faith: until he realizes that there is a spiritual law in his own make-up which will operate if he will put it in the way of operating. He who understands this law *rejoices whilst yet in captivity,* because he can see with his "inner eye" the glorious picture of the promised land. In this way the three kings rejoiced whilst yet in captivity to the drought of the desert, because Elisha showed them the promise of rain as the fulfilment of faith. In this way a man must always see the goal from

---

* Numbers 13 : 33.

the very beginning and hold to the vision with unswerving loyalty and faith. In this way he may *demand* the visible manifestation of that good thing which he has already received on the invisible plane.

Jesus Christ gave us a wonderful piece of advice in regard to this principle of life. He said to his disciples, *Say not ye, There are yet four months and then cometh harvest? behold, I say unto you, Lift up your eyes, and look on the fields; for they are white already to harvest.** Christ was not the sentimental figure that has been made of Him by the world's misunderstanding. His clear vision saw the so-called material world in a manner quite different from that in which we see it. He saw what we may call the fourth dimensional world, which Einstein has but inadequately described in mathematical form. Jesus saw things as they really are in the Universal Mind; perfect and complete.

Jesus was trying to show his disciples that God has already provided for man more than enough, but He always taught that this provision did not take shape in a man's experience until that man had taken the first step and thereby proved his sincerity. *Ask, and it shall be given you; seek, and ye shall find; knock, and it shall be opened unto you.*† The promise of the great Nazarene was explicit enough. True prayer consists of putting yourself into tune with the Universal Mind: for whereas so many

* John 4 : 35.   † Matthew 7 : 7.

people think that prayer is the art of getting
God to *give* something, it is actually the art of
getting yourself ready to *receive* something.

It is your own insufficiency that stands
between you and your ideals and your heart's
desire. It is your fear that blocks the way.
Jesus said, *Why are ye fearful, O ye of little
faith?** and was always more ready to blame
His disciples for their insufficiency when they
failed to heal or to cast out devils (as healing the insane was called) than He was
given to sympathizing with them for any
helplessness.

*When you can wish without worrying, every desire
of your heart will be immediately fulfilled*—though
here let me warn you that I have more to say
on this subject before I close, for do not make
the mistake of supposing that you can just
demand and receive, to consume the gift upon
your lusts; for Jesus pointed out that abuse of
the law led to failure.

In the Yoga philosophy we have a great
saying: you will read it on page 153 of my book
THE INVISIBLE INFLUENCE†—the book which
will change your whole attitude towards life.
Let me quote to you a few words of what the
Great Lhama said to me as I passed from his
presence. *Fear not any man,* he said in a slow
but forceful undertone. *Fear not thineself;
remember that fear is failure and the forerunner of*

* Matthew 8 : 26.
† Published by Rider & Co., London, 5s. net.

failure. Be thou therefore without fear, for in the heart of the coward virtue abideth not.

At the present time we are nearly all of us slaves to fear. But the day will dawn, and that day is not far distant, when men will realize that they are in themselves the generators of good and evil, and that the evil they fear is born by them of that fear. Then man will consciously take hold upon his own destiny. He will see that he is indeed the master of his fate and the captain of his soul. His release from bondage will come in a flash. The present earth will then truly pass away and each one, individually and collectively, will find himself to be living in a new heaven and a new earth.

And I saw a new heaven and a new earth . . . and there shall be no more death, neither sorrow, nor crying, neither shall there be any more pain: for the former things are passed away. * This vision foresaw the domination of mind over matter, the secret of which the Aryan Hindoos have known for more than three thousand years.

There is nothing new about this idea of the universe. The law of God has been the same and will remain the same for all time and eternity. There never has existed in the Universal Mind any death, sorrow, suffering, weeping, anguish or pain. These things are due to the fact that our "little cups of water," in which we reflect God, are muddy and impure

---

* Revelation 21 : 4.

through the admixture of fear and our own limitations. It is up to us to understand what we mean by that reflection and to clear our own instruments of their impurity. To do this we must stand guard at the gates of our own thoughts so that nothing in the way of evil or negative thoughts shall sink down into our unconscious mind. If they are allowed to do so they will breed, and breed, and attract other like forces to them. Did not Paul say, *We wrestle not against flesh and blood, but against principalities, against powers, against the rulers of the darkness of this world.** Birds of a feather flock together! Like attracts like! If your thoughts are evil or fearful you are hanging out a sign in the Invisible World that will attract the evil powers just as surely as the vultures are attracted to the carrion. Everything in the universe consists of vibrations. Your thoughts are vibrations, and they will not be picked up by those persons and powers whose "wavelength" is not yours. Think evil and you will attract evil people. Think good and you will attract good people.

I realize that I am using the terms Conscious mind, Subconscious mind, and Unconscious mind pretty freely, and I am beginning to wonder whether you understand exactly how I am using them. Let me describe briefly to you what I mean by these different "levels" of thought. Let us take an example of their

---

* Ephesians 6 : 12.

functions to illustrate what they are. I look at the clock and observe that it is five o'clock: my *conscious mind* has made an observation. The thought is not lost, but it passes into my *subconscious mind* and there it finds an answering echo from a conscious thought I had made the day before when I told my colleague to meet me at five-thirty. (The contents of my subconscious mind can be recalled by a slight association but not so with the unconscious mind.) This reawakening of an echo I call "remembering," and yet I find that, even though I may have forgotten all about the appointment with my colleague in twenty, thirty, forty or more years ahead, I can, by being deeply hypnotized, be made to remember every incident of my life—even to such a detail as looking at the clock and remembering my rendezvous with a colleague, although it has now sunk down into the depths of my unconscious mind. The *unconscious mind* keeps within its depths the secrets I have long forgotten, and perhaps it even holds the secret of life itself. It is like a delicate gramophone record of incredible capacity: every fleeting thought is registered by it, and in its depths, by the subtle connection between it and the Universal Mind, each thought re-echoes upon the very walls of Time into Eternity. Realize this! Think what it means! Your thoughts are your constant prayer to, or your constant rejection of, God. You are building up a great library of your own deeds—a great autobiography which no amount of lies can ever hide from you at last. This is the record, the Silent Listener, which every man bears in his bosom, and this is the basis of the old stories about the Recording Angel, and his Golden Pen, and his Doomsday Book. Of a truth this is no exaggeration—no fairy story: the Creator knows the fall of every sparrow through the Universal Mind: do you suppose that your smallest thought is missed? No! It is penned against you, and though you may hide your thoughts from the world, the unseen law of Karma will weigh its forces for or against you in the end, and you will receive the blessing of God, or know the full horror of separation from Him—separation by your own hand from the very source of your being.

Now, if your unuttered and unmanifested thought can have such tremendous effects, does it not follow that your uttered thought will be doubly powerful? In the twenty-first verse of the eighteenth chapter of Proverbs we read, *Death and life are in the power of the tongue.* Just remember this fact and be doubly careful of the words you use, for how many a man has ruined his whole life by an idle word? The whole force of your desire becomes immeasurably heightened when you not only utter your desire, but when you also obtain the agreement of another person. Jesus, the great Nazarene Yogi, knew this to be true, for He said: *If two of you shall agree on earth as touching any thing that* *they shall ask, it shall be done for them of my Father which is in heaven** This being true, you should not only trust in God, the Giver, and also the Gift, but you should also trust in yourself, the asker, and the recipient, and in other men who must in the end support you in your right desire. Yes! All men must in the end support you if your desire be right and true, for in the Bible we read: *Surely the wrath of man shall praise thee: the remainder of wrath shalt thou restrain.*†

Testimony is paid to the power of thought even by those childish people who put their faith in horseshoes and such talismen. For it is their faith, pinned to the symbol, which gives the horseshoe power to those who believe in it. As an illustration of this let us look back a few years to the time when our grandfathers were much intrigued by the magic rods which a certain American gentleman brought to this country and sold by the hundred at a fat price per pair. These rods were guaranteed to cure all ills, and so well did they do their task that their manufacturer and purveyor became extremely wealthy, and was, moreover, lauded in Pulpit and Press as a public benefactor. This went on until a little group of doctors made up a few sets of these rods from common everyday materials, and, passing them off as genuine, yet obtained exactly the same cures. With this evidence they stopped the sale of the rods

---

* Matthew 18 : 19.   † Psalms 76 : 10.

and sent the American back home (with a fortune), and completely broke the "healing power" of the rods. Does this not prove the power of thought and faith to attach themselves to ordinary material objects? Does it not explain the mysterious power of shrines and ikons the world over? Moreover, is it not strange that people, having had such a convincing demonstration of the power of thought, should go back to their ills and their fears? Saying of the rods, " It was *only* faith after all." ONLY FAITH! One might as well dismiss a thunderstorm as of no importance by calling it *only a discharge of electricity!*

Only faith! Faith is everything in your life! *Eliminate faith from life and what remains?* Little or nothing that matters! *Keep* your faith, and the substance of your faith will come to you, for faith *is* the substance of things hoped for. Cast off fear and begin to live as though you knew the truth of this! Go on with the task of putting yourself in order first, knowing that the things needed to manifest perfection in this world are ready and waiting for you in the unseen world. These things will come to you if you act in the way to prepare for them. *In due season we shall reap, if we faint not.** Keep up the chin! Keep the flame of faith alive! Paint your house and keep it in good repair as though you were of some account, and the needs you have demonstrated *will* be met!

---

* Galatians 6 : 9.

HOW TO GET WHAT YOU WANT   45

Don't run away with the false impression that this is some silly make-believe, and that all you have to do to get a motor-car, for example, is to rent a garage. There must be some real need and some real meaning to your desire, and a real faith in your need and your God. Yet even what you may call "make-believe" will impress the unconscious mind in a most telling way. I know of a girl whose mother was at her wits' end because, although they were very poor, the girl was always talking and thinking of rings and things. *She never envied others*, but she lived in a world of wonders, and riches seemed real to her. One day, quite out of the blue, a wealthy man walked into the shop where she was employed and fell in love with her. Later she married him and her dreams came true. You may call that a child's outlook on life, but don't forget that Jesus Christ said: *Whosoever shall not receive the kingdom of God as a little child, he shall not enter therein.* *

Therefore, I say to you: Dream of a great future and that future will come to you! For *All things are possible to him that believeth.*† Fear will vanish when you walk up to it and face it like a man. The lion takes its fierceness from your fear: walk up to him and he will run from you; run away from him and he will run *after* you. Banish fear and you also banish evil. Love one another and hate will be no more.

---

* Mark 10 : 15.   † Mark 9 : 23.

Face a situation fearlessly and there is no situation to be faced. We often hear people talking about getting people to "pull the strings for them," but we may indeed wonder why they need to enlist such comparatively puerile help when, all around, never sleeping, never failing, there is this great Invisible Influence "pulling the strings" in the unseen world—those delicate, cosmic springs of life. Every word and every thought is an unseen vibratory "string" which "pulls" forces into operation in the unseen world. Think health, good, wealth, and happiness, and these things will come to you without getting anyone to "pull strings" for you. Think sickness, evil, poverty, and despair, and you will get them, even though all the King's horses and all the King's men are busy "pulling strings" for you.

Never despise the day of small things! Don't be a spiritual snob! Cast your whole energy into loving the little things as well as the big ones, for the little things presage greater ones ahead. You will get little signs of the Promised Land long before you see it. Before Christopher Columbus reached the great continent of America, he saw birds in the air, and twigs in the water which told him that his great day was near. So it is with your life!

The law of *Karma* applies with equal force to the lives of nations. Sometimes it takes time to act, but it never fails to do so. Take the case of America and France. During the War of Independence, France sent help to America; La Fayette and his friends sailed to the help of the struggling colonists. Over one hundred years rolled by, and there came a day when the Great War had been raging for four terrible years, and the Allies were on their last beam— to be candid, we thought we had lost the war. We who were out in France were wondering how to get the troops out of the Continent with the least possible loss of life, for we saw that our only hope would bê to rely upon the British Navy. In London the news was received by a thoroughly "blue" parliament. The message had also gone across the seas to America; but another message had gone with it on the unseen wires of *Karma*; the reminder of the unpaid debt of honour which America owed to France. In the Capitol at Washington, D.C., amid a silence whose depth it is beyond my words to convey, the late President Woodrow Wilson rose to his feet and read the message to Congress: "Send us plenty of men and munitions and we shall win." The hand of fate was over the vast continent of America. The "strings" had been "pulled" on the unseen plane: La Fayette and his brothers reached ghostly hands back over the century agone and signed the American declaration of War on Germany. And so America sent help to France. The law may take a long time to operate, but what is put into the world will again come out of it.

And now it is time to tell you of another law whose operation is bound up with that of the law of *Karma*: this is called the Law of Substitution. It is the law which assures that what you get is not what you want but what you deserve. Jesus plainly said that a man sometimes does not get what he wants because he asks amiss so that he may consume it upon his lusts. Imagine what a ghastly holocaust there would be if the thing were as simple as all that: if every thing that was wanted, even though it were not definitely evil, came in the way in which it was demanded. No, it is not the mere word of prayer that connects you with the Great Giver; it is your unwritten thoughts and your carefully recorded worth.

Many a young man has found himself in love, and has wished for the consummation of his heart's desire, but somehow there has always been some difficulty in the way. I am often asked to help people in love (yes, I get quite a lot of letters to that effect), but all I would ever consent to do would be to help you to get into that relation with the Universal Mind which will impel you to marry the right person. I would not take upon myself the responsibility of deciding what was right for you. Maybe you will find, if you do as I say, that the object of your affections does not come up to your expectations after all. You begin to question whether you have experienced a divine selection, after all. Later on you meet someone else who proves to be your absolute ideal, and then you say it is uncanny. I say it is not in the least uncanny—you are experiencing the operation of the law of Substitution.

If you had fought and scrambled to bolster up the false situation with the first person, you would never have found the real one; and this is why masterly inactivity is sometimes the way to success. There is such a thing as the law of non-resistance. *"Resist not evil,"** we are told: *"Be not overcome of evil, but overcome evil with good."*† Resistance is hell, for it places a man in a state of torment. The Chinese tell you that water is the most powerful element in the world because it is absolutely non-resistant. It will find a way in where more direct forces would be powerless. It gives way before pressure, but in the end it will affect the thing that presses it. Dropping water wears away a rock.

These are great magic laws of which I have told you. The law of opulence, of substitution of health, of non-resistance—*Karma* with intuition and divine guidance. But there is a greater law than all these, and in which they are all contained. This law is the Law of Love. *In all thy ways acknowledge Him, and He shall direct thy paths.*‡ In business, in pleasure, in every walk of life, however high or however low, we can never get away from the truth of the Gospel of Jesus Christ. For that gospel is one of

---

* Matthew 5 : 39.   † Romans 12 : 21.   ‡ Proverbs 3 : 6.

supreme love. It does not permit the entrance of any selfish thing. It does not permit a mere selfish getting, but balances a just account of giving and receiving.

A relative of mine used to say, *We gather whilst they scatter.* But what a misunderstanding this is of the great Law of Life; for this is not an interpretation of brotherhood, it is merely a selfish doctrine presented in Biblical terms. For there is a direct counter to such a false presentation of the Law of Life which says, *There is that scattereth, and yet increaseth; and there is that withholdeth more than is meet, but it tendeth to poverty.**

This last is the law of a generous God for all men of generous minds, and it is clearly laid down in that greatest of all law-books; which is also a great scientific text-book, and a great story-book too.

You know well enough the book to which I refer. It is THE HOLY BIBLE, and I cannot do better than to close this talk with a passage from its pages which is indeed the keynote of my subject: *Seek ye* FIRST *the kingdom of God, and his righteousness, and all these things* (health, wealth and happiness) *shall be added unto you.*†

---

* Proverbs 11 : 24.   † Matthew 6 : 33.

APPENDIX A.

During the course of this lecture at the Mayfair Hotel, the announcement was made that a Medium to whom I had only recently been introduced, would take the platform and would go under control at 5.30, and the lecture would thereupon have to be abandoned for a short while to allow the public to see the Medium at work.

The Medium, a young man from Chiswick, a stoker by trade, then ascended the platform accompanied by a friend who had sponsored him. This friend, who had been a violinist, had lost the power of her arms and hands, but, by the treatment received through the Medium from a doctor alleged to be still living in Thibet, was gradually regaining the use of her arms.

The Medium sat on a vacant chair beside his friend, and the author went on with his lecture. Within one minute of 5.30 the Medium suddenly went under control, and began to speak English with an Eastern accent, assuming a mien quite out of keeping with his usual retiring disposition. Addressing the woman by his side as "Nurse," he began in a most imperious manner to order her to bring "patient number one" for his treatment. This she did (the patient being herself), whereupon he seized her arm in a most professional manner and began to perform a most able feat of manipulative surgery. Several doctors were on the platform, and they were amazed by the skill manifested by the Medium.

During this demonstration a most amazing occurrence took place in the audience. At a table near the platform sat a party of friends, including among their number Mr. Frank Leah, the well-known Artist and Sensitive. This latter gentleman was seen to be in great pain, holding his arms and making every attempt to massage his wrists. Eventually he had to retire until the performance was over. Questioned after this event, Mr. Leah stated that he could feel the mental radiations of disease which lay at the back of the woman's physical condition. Although this was unknown to the audience, it would, had it been known, have added considerable evidential weight to my insistence upon the wholly mental nature of disease.

After finishing his demonstration of manipulative surgery, the Medium then was questioned by me. I asked him very deliberate questions in a loud voice so that the whole room could hear, and also repeated the Medium's replies in a like manner.

The Medium answered the questions in an imperious voice and became annoyed by my insistence on behalf of the audience. "Can't you understand, confound you!" he broke out angrily upon several occasions.

The most interesting information given by the Medium was to the effect that Sound, Light, and Perfume were all curative agents in the order of importance given, and that the co-incidence of the three vibratory media could be effected with very beneficial results. He also told me that march tunes are the best for calming distraught minds.

In reply to the question Where do you get this information? the Medium replied testily, "Confound you, I get it from my great Master, Pythagoras, who taught all there is to know about vibrations."

The information was scanty owing to frequent interruptions, and by the fact the Medium went out of control shortly after I had begun to ply him with deliberate questions.

I have since seen the same Medium under control of an entity who claimed to be the Master of the White Lodge. Strangely and interestingly enough, when so controlled the Medium always gives the true Yogi sign.

APPENDIX B.

After the lecture, a demonstration of the principles upon which levitation is based was given. Miss Kyra Nijinski, daughter of the famous dancer, was the subject, and although levitation did not actually take place, the body of the girl became raised to a pitch quite unattainable by any gymnastic means. Certain sections of the Press reported unfavourably on the incident, but the following resumé was afterwards made of opinions which came into my hands or into the hands of my publishers.

COMMENTS ON THE LEVITATION DEMONSTRATION

Dr. John Cunningham Duncanson, of the Ministry of Health and late Medical Adviser to the Borough Council of Woolwich, states that he saw the demonstration of the principles of levitation at the Mayfair Hotel Tea-Talk on March 25th by Dr. Alexander Cannon. He says: "The result was to my mind most impressive and I entirely disagree with the remark in the Press of the 26th March that all that was achieved was a difficult gymnastic feat. I am myself an old gymnastic champion and a medical man."

Dr. Thos. Mather Thomson, the radiation scientist and late professor (assistant) in Dublin, states that he is prepared to vouch for the fact that the subject at one point not only raised her head and chest from the ground, but also her hips by two inches, and, in fact, was commencing to levitate.

Mrs. Marie Freeman, the psychist of Knightsbridge, states that Dr. Alexander Cannon handed over to her for psychic training Miss Kyra Nijinski, the daughter of the famous dancer, who performed the feat on March the 25th at the Mayfair Hotel and that she has been actually levitated to the ceiling by the use of certain body vibrations used in the trance state.

Dr. Nandor Fordor lectured on "The Problem of Human Levitation" at the British College of Psychic Science on May the 31st, 1933, giving very convincing proof of the existence of this great feat defying all the known laws of Gravity. His lecture is published in the April number of the Quarterly Transactions of the College this year. Amongst the people who have been levitated are: St. Dunstan; St. Dominic; St. Francis of Assisi; St. Thomas Aquinas; St. Edmund, Archbishop of Canterbury; Blessed James of Illyria; Savonarola; St. Ignatius Loyola; St. Phillip Neri; St. Peter of Alcantara; St. Joseph of

Copertino; St. Alphonso Liguori; Gegenwart of Vienna; Abbé Petit; Henry Jones; Patrick Sandilands; Mary London; The Drummer of Tedworth; Nancy Wesley (during John Wesley's troubles at Epworth Vicarage); Harry Phelps; Henry Gordon; D. D. Home; Victoria Claire of Coux; Mrs. Volckman Zucarini; M. C., the sculptor; Robert Bell; Cecil Husk; Eglinton (in the presence of the Emperor and the Empress of Russia, the Grand Duke of Oldenburg and the Grand Duke Vladimir); Ruggieri; Ira, William and Elizabeth Davenport; Maria Vollhardt; Willy Schneider; Carlos Mirabelli; Covindassamy; Dr. Cannon and others.

APPENDIX C

During the writing of this volume there came into my hands a copy of THE NEWS CHRONICLE dated July 3rd, 1934, in which was printed an article by Mr. Hugh Redwood, entitled DO YOU BELIEVE IN PRAYER.

Mr. Redwood reproduces there some of the letters which have come to him, and by the courtesy of the Editor of THE NEWS CHRONICLE I am enabled again to reproduce them for your benefit. True, they are not more spectacular than some of the instances quoted by myself, but there is always an added interest in a testimony when other, and disinterested, testimony is conjoined.

Mr. Redwood tells how The Missionary Training Colony, Highfield Hill, Upper Norwood, had £8 of bills to meet and nothing in hand to meet them with. The men who ran it were convinced that God would aid them, and they would, therefore, neither run into debt nor issue a public appeal. Instead of this it cancelled its standing orders with the local tradespeople and waited. Here is the result:

By 9.30 a.m. a baker seven miles away, who was unknown to us, phoned, to say he had ninety-two large loaves made in error—could we use them? The evening post brought in £8 (within 3d.), and the next morning the first cheque of £25 received for three months met the rates.

Mr. Redwood also quotes from a letter written to him by Mr. Shearman, the evangelistic secretary of The Bible School and Missionary Association, Hampstead.

It is a rule of our work never to ask for money, but to leave our needs with God. Many times we have been in difficult places, but we have always been delivered.

One of the most notable instances occurred when, with only £200 in the bank, we had faith to purchase a church for £1,700. The amount in hand was paid as deposit, and the time came when it would be forfeited if the balance were not forthcoming on the morrow.

At bedtime no money had arrived, but the matter was completely committed to God, and Mr. Carter was about to retire for the night when he saw something lying on the front-door mat. As it seemed to be nothing but an advertisement in a cheap-looking envelope his impulse was to leave it there, but on second thoughts he picked it up.

It proved to contain £1,000 in notes, without a single word of explanation. The remaining £500 arrived the next morning, while the completion of the purchase was being hela up at the solicitor's office for the want of it.

Could there, indeed, be more striking confirmation than this of the truth of the command to the Three Kings in the desert? That school which cancelled its standing orders and waited for God to act was obeying the command to act in confidence: *Thus saith the law, ye shall not see wind, neither shall ye see rain, yet make this valley full of ditches.*

Note carefully, however, that all these people were filled with a sense of purpose in life. They did not ask for Rolls Royces and a life of ease—imagine the folly of supposing that the Law has any concern with that sort of thing! No, the life that harnesses the power of the Law is the life that is dedicated to the mission of Truth in some degree, and which can rightly call upon the Fatherhood of God for support.

This is the end of this publication.

Any remaining blank pages are for our book binding requirements and are blank on purpose.

To search thousands of interesting publications like this one, please remember to visit our website at:

http://www.kessinger.net

CPSIA information can be obtained
at www.ICGtesting.com
Printed in the USA
BVHW041033291121
622769BV00016B/767